Pebble® Plus

ALL ABOUT WINTER

Animals in Winter

by Martha E. H. Rustad

Consulting Editor: Gail Saunders-Smith, PhD

Capstone press®

Mankato, Minnesota

Pebble Plus is published by Capstone Press,
151 Good Counsel Drive, P.O. Box 669, Mankato, Minnesota 56002.
www.capstonepress.com

1 2 3 4 5 6 13 12 11 10 09 08

Library of Congress Cataloging-in-Publication Data
Rustad, Martha E. H. (Martha Elizabeth Hillman), 1975–
    Animals in winter / by Martha E. H. Rustad.
    p. cm. — (Pebble plus. All about winter)
    Summary: "Simple text and photographs present animals in winter" — Provided by publisher.
    Includes bibliographical references and index.
    ISBN-13: 978-1-4296-2200-4 (hardcover)
    ISBN-10: 1-4296-2200-8 (hardcover)
    1. Animal behavior — Juvenile literature. 2. Winter — Juvenile literature. I. Title. II. Series.
QL751.5.R88 2009
578.4'3 — dc22   2008003253

Editorial Credits
Sarah L. Schuette, editor; Veronica Bianchini, designer; Jo Miller and Marcie Spence, photo researchers

Photo Credits
Bruce Coleman Inc./Jaanus Jarva, 9; Kerry Givens, 13
Capstone Press/Karon Dubke, 15
Dreamstime/Misscanon, cover
iStockphoto/lightstalker, 5
Peter Arnold/Walter H. Hodge, 21
Shutterstock/Graham Tomlin, 1; Joy Brown, 7; Susan Kehoe, 11
SuperStock Inc., 17; Tom Brakefield, 19

Note to Parents and Teachers

The All about Winter set supports national science standards related to changes during
the seasons. This book describes and illustrates animals in winter. The images support
early readers in understanding the text. The repetition of words and phrases helps early
readers learn new words. This book also introduces early readers to subject-specific
vocabulary words, which are defined in the Glossary section. Early readers may need
assistance to read some words and to use the Table of Contents, Glossary, Read More,
Internet Sites, and Index sections of the book.

Table of Contents

Winter Is Here

It's winter.
Animals do many things
to survive
the cold temperatures.

Migration

Some animals migrate
to warmer places for winter.
Birds fly together
to their winter home.

Reindeer walk far
to find food.
They dig to find berries
and grass under the snow.

Hibernation

Black bears hibernate
alone in their dens.
Their thick fur
keeps them warm.

Groups of bats
hibernate together.
They hang upside down close
together to stay warm.

Other Animals

Fish spend the winter
near the bottom of lakes.
They wait for the ice to melt
in the spring.

Squirrels hide nuts in the fall.

Then they find and eat

the nuts in winter.

Snowshoe hares hop through snow on their long feet. Their white winter fur helps them hide from predators.

Signs of Winter

Animals on the move
leave tracks in the snow.
What are other signs
of animals in winter?

Glossary

den — a place where a wild animal lives; a den may be a hole in the ground, a cave, or tree trunk.

hibernate — to spend winter in a sleepy resting state without much activity

migrate — to move or fly to a different place because of the weather

predator — an animal that hunts another animal for food

survive — to stay alive through a dangerous or other event

temperature — the measure of how hot or cold something is

Read More

Hall, Margaret. *Hibernation.* Patterns in Nature. Mankato, Minn.: Capstone Press, 2007.

Higginson, Mel. *Migration.* Nature's Cycle. Vero Beach, Fla.: Rourke, 2007.

Latta, Sara L. *What Happens in Winter?* I Like the Seasons. Berkeley Heights, N.J.: Enslow, 2006.

Internet Sites

FactHound offers a safe, fun way to find Internet sites related to this book. All of the sites on FactHound have been researched by our staff.

Here's how:

1. Visit *www.facthound.com*

2. Choose your grade level.

3. Type in this book ID **1429622008** for age-appropriate sites. You may also browse subjects by clicking on letters, or by clicking on pictures and words.

4. Click on the **Fetch It** button.

FactHound will fetch the best sites for you!

Index

Word Count: 138
Grade: 1
Early-Intervention Level: 16